ASTROLOGY
SELF-CARE

Gemini

ASTROLOGY
SELF-CARE

Gemini

Live your best life
by the stars

Sarah Bartlett

First published in Great Britain in 2022 by Yellow Kite
An imprint of Hodder & Stoughton
An Hachette UK company

1

Illustrations © shutterstock.com

A CIP catalogue record for this title is
available from the British Library

Hardback ISBN 978 1 399 70464 9
eBook ISBN 978 1 399 70466 3
Audiobook ISBN 978 1 399 70465 6

Designed by Goldust Design

Typeset in Nocturne Serif by Hewer Text UK Ltd, Edinburgh
Printed and bound in Great Britain by Clays Ltd, Elcograf S.p.A.

Hodder & Stoughton policy is to use papers that are
natural, renewable and recyclable products and made
from wood grown in sustainable forests. The logging and
manufacturing processes are expected to conform to the
environmental regulations of the country of origin.

Yellow Kite
Hodder & Stoughton Ltd
Carmelite House
50 Victoria Embankment
London EC4Y 0DZ

www.yellowkitebooks.co.uk

*Those who cannot change their
minds cannot change anything.*

George Bernard Shaw, playwright

There is a path, hidden between the road of reason and the hedgerow of dreams, which leads to the secret garden of self-knowledge. This book will show you the way.

Contents

Introduction

The ancient Greek goddess Gaia arose from Chaos and was the personification of the Earth and all of Nature. One of the first primordial beings, along with Tartarus (the Underworld), Eros (love) and Nyx (night), as mother of all life, she is both the embodiment of all that this planet is and its spiritual caretaker.

It's hardly likely you will want to become a full-time Mother Earth, but many of us right now are caring more about our beautiful planet and all that lives upon it. To nurture and respect this amazing place we call home, and to preserve this tiny dot in the Universe, the best place to start is, well, with you.

Self-care is about respecting and honouring who you are as an individual. It's about realising that nurturing yourself is neither vanity nor a conceit, but a creative act that brings an awesome sense of awareness and a deeper connection to the Universe and all that's in it. Caring about yourself means you care about everything in the cosmos – because you are part of it.

But self-care isn't just about trekking to the gym, jogging around the park or eating the right foods. It's also about discovering who you are becoming as an individual and caring for that authenticity (and loving and caring about who we are becoming means others can love and care about us, too). This is where the art of sun-sign astrology comes in.

Astrology and Self-Care

So what is astrology? And how can it direct each of us to the right self-care pathway? Put simply, astrology is the study of the planets, sun and moon and their influence on events and people here on Earth. It is an art that has been used for thousands of years to forecast world events, military and political outcomes and, more recently, financial market trends. As such, it is an invaluable tool for understanding our own individuality and how to be true to ourselves. Although there is still dispute within astrological circles as to whether the planets actually physically affect us, there is strong evidence to show that the cycles and patterns they create in the sky have a direct mirroring effect on what happens down here on Earth and, more importantly, on each individual's personality.

Your horoscope or birth-chart is a snapshot of the planets, sun and moon in the sky at the moment you were born. This amazing picture reveals all your innate potential, characteristics and qualities. In fact, it is probably the best 'selfie' you could ever have! Astrology can not only tell you who you are, but also how best to care for that self and your own specific needs and desires as revealed by your birth-chart.

Self-care is simply time to look after yourself – to restore, inspirit and refresh and love your unique self. But it's also about understanding, accepting and

11

being aware of your own traits – both the good and not so good – so that you can then say, 'It's ok to be me, and my intention is to become the best of myself'. In fact, by looking up to the stars and seeing how they reflect us down here on Earth, we can deepen our connection to the Universe for the good of all, too. Understanding that caring about ourselves is not selfish creates an awesome sense of self-acceptance and awareness.

So how does each of us honour the individual 'me' and find the right kind of rituals and practices to suit our personalities? Astrology sorts us out into the zodiac – an imaginary belt encircling the Earth divided into twelve sun signs; so, for example, what one sign finds relaxing, another may find a hassle or stressful. When it comes to physical fitness, adventurous Arians thrive on aerobic work, while soulful Pisceans feel nurtured by yoga. Financial reward or status would inspire the ambitious Capricorn mind, while theatrical Leos need to indulge their joy of being centre stage.

By knowing which sun sign you are and its associated characteristics, you will discover the right self-care routines and practices to suit you. And this unique and empowering book is here to help – with all the rituals and practices in these pages specifically suited to your sun-sign personality for nurturing and vitalising your mind, body and spirit.

However, self-care is not an excuse to be lazy and avoid the goings on in the rest of the world. Self-care is about taking responsibility for our choices and understanding our unique essence, so that we can engage with all aspects of ourselves and the way we interact with the world.

IN A NUTSHELL

The mercurial motivation to adapt and develop all aspects of your powers of communication and knowledge means you excel at mindful self-care, such as enhancing your intuition, understanding your psyche and nurturing your seductive streak. Use this book as a guide to other forms of care, too, such as restoring physical equilibrium, looking your best and expressing the playful nature of the Gemini twins. There are no set routines, only inspirational practices to help you understand yourself and realise you have every right to be as light-hearted, fun-loving and carefree as you want to be. This, in itself, is another way to discover who you are truly becoming.

Sun-Sign Astrology

Also known as your star sign or zodiac sign, your sun sign encompasses the following:

* Your solar identity, or sense of self
* What really matters to you
* Your future intentions
* Your sense of purpose
* Various qualities that manifest through your actions, goals, desires and the personal sense of being 'you'
* Your sense of being 'centred' – whether 'self-centred' (too much ego) or 'self-conscious' (too little ego); in other words, how you perceive who you are as an individual

In fact, the sun tells you how you can 'shine' best to become who you really are.

ASTROLOGY FACTS

The zodiac or sun signs are twelve 30-degree segments that create an imaginary belt around the Earth. The zodiac belt is also known as the ecliptic, which is the apparent path of the sun as it travels round the Earth during the year.

The sun or zodiac signs are further divided into four elements (Fire, Earth, Air and Water, denoting a certain energy ruling each sign), plus three modalities (qualities associated with how we interact with the world; these are known as Cardinal, Fixed and Mutable). So as a Gemini, for example, you are a 'Mutable Air' sign.

* Fire signs: Aries, Leo, Sagittarius
  They are: extrovert, passionate, assertive

* Earth signs: Taurus, Virgo, Capricorn
  They are: practical, materialistic, sensual

* Air signs: Gemini, Libra, Aquarius
  They are: communicative, innovative, inquisitive

* Water signs: Cancer, Scorpio, Pisces
  They are: emotional, intuitive, understanding

The modalities are based on their seasonal resonance according to the northern hemisphere.

Cardinal signs instigate and initiate ideas and projects.
They are: Aries, Cancer, Libra and Capricorn

Fixed signs resolutely build and shape ideas.
They are: Taurus, Leo, Scorpio and Aquarius

Mutable signs generate creative change and adapt ideas to reach a conclusion.

They are: Gemini, Virgo, Sagittarius and Pisces

Planetary rulers

Each zodiac sign is assigned a planet, which highlights the qualities of that sign:

Aries is ruled by Mars (fearless)
Taurus is ruled by Venus (indulgent)
Gemini is ruled by Mercury (magical)
Cancer is ruled by the moon (instinctive)
Leo is ruled by the sun (empowering)
Virgo is ruled by Mercury (informative)
Libra is ruled by Venus (compassionate)
Scorpio is ruled by Pluto (passionate)
Sagittarius is ruled by Jupiter (adventurous)
Capricorn is ruled by Saturn (disciplined)
Aquarius is ruled by Uranus (innovative)
Pisces is ruled by Neptune (imaginative)

Opposite Signs

Signs oppose one another across the zodiac (i.e. those that are 180 degrees away from each other) – for example, Gemini opposes Sagittarius and Taurus opposes Scorpio. We often find ourselves mysteriously attracted to our opposite signs in romantic relationships, and while the signs' traits appear to clash in this 'polarity', the essence of each is contained in the other (note, they have the same modality). Gaining insight into the characteristics of your opposite sign (which are, essentially, inherent in you) can deepen your understanding of the energetic interplay of the horoscope.

On The Cusp

Some of us are born 'on the cusp' of two signs – in other words, the day or time when the sun moved from one zodiac sign to another. If you were born at the end or beginning of the dates usually given in horoscope pages (the sun's move through one sign usually lasts approximately four weeks), you can check which sign you are by contacting a reputable astrologer (or astrology site) (see Resources, p. 117) who will calculate it exactly for you. For example, 23 August is the standardised changeover day for the sun to move into Virgo and out of Leo. But every year, the time and even sometimes the day the sun changes sign can differ. So, say you were born on 23 August at five in the morning and the sun didn't move into Virgo until five in the afternoon on that day, you would be a Leo, not a Virgo.

How To Use This Book

The book is divided into three parts, each guiding you in applying self-care to different areas of your life:

* Part One: your mind and feelings
* Part Two: your body
* Part Three: your soul

Caring about the mind using rituals or ideas tailored to your sign shows you ways to unlock stress, restore focus or widen your perception. Applying the practices in Part One will connect you to your feelings and help you to acknowledge and become aware of why your emotions are as they are and how to deal with them. This sort of emotional self-care will set you up to deal with your relationships better, enhance all forms of communication and ensure you know exactly how to ask for what you want or need, and be true to your deepest desires.

A WORD ON CHAKRAS

Eastern spiritual traditions maintain that universal energy, known as 'prana' in India and 'chi' in Chinese philosophy, flows through the body, linked by seven subtle energy centres known as chakras (Sanskrit for 'wheel'). These energies are believed to revolve or spiral around and through our bodies, vibrating at different frequencies (corresponding to seven colours of the light spectrum) in an upward, vertical direction. Specific crystals are placed on the chakras to heal, harmonise, stimulate or subdue the chakras if imbalance is found.

The seven chakras are:
* The base or root (found at the base of the spine)
* The sacral (mid-belly)
* The solar plexus (between belly and chest)
* The heart (centre of chest)
* The throat (throat)
* The third eye (between the eyebrows)
* The crown (top of the head)

On p. 87 we will look in more detail at how Geminis can work with chakras for self-care.

Fitness and caring for the body are different for all of us, too. While Gemini benefits from daily stretching or breathwork, for example, Taurus thrives on aromatherapy sessions and Aquarius a good hike. Delve into Part Two whenever you're in need of physical restoration or a sensual makeover tailored to your sign.

Spiritual self-care opens you to your sacred self or soul. Which is why Part Three looks at how you can nurture your soul according to your astrological sun sign. It shows you how to connect to and care for your spirituality in simple ways, such as being at one with Nature or just enjoying the world around you. It will show you how to be more positive about who you are and honour your connection to the Universe. In fact, all the rituals and practices in this section will bring you joyful relating, harmonious living and a true sense of happiness.

The Key

Remember, your birth-chart or horoscope is like the key to a treasure chest containing the most precious jewels that make you you. Learn about them, and care for them well. Use this book to polish, nurture, respect and give value to the beautiful gemstones of who you are, and, in doing so, bring your potential to life. It's your right to be true to who you are, just by virtue of being born on this planet, and therefore being a child of Mother Earth and the cosmos.

Care for you, and you care for the Universe.

GEMINI
WORDS OF WISDOM

As you embark on your self-care journey, it's important to look at the lunar cycles and specific astrological moments throughout the year. At those times (and, indeed, at any time you choose), the words of Gemini wisdom below will be invaluable, empowering you with positive energy. Taking a few mindful moments at each of the four major phases of every lunar cycle and at the two important astrological moments in your solar year (see Glossary, p. 119) will affirm and enhance your positive attitude towards caring about yourself and the world.

NEW CRESCENT MOON – to care for yourself:

'An oracle is a message from the gods or the Universe, from all that is already known and will be known. If I listen to the message, it will show me the way.'

'I bring joy to myself and those around me by being who I am.'

'I believe in all my skills and trust in my talents.'

FULL MOON – for sealing your intention to care for your feeling world:

'I can feel warmth, happiness and love when I care for who I am.'

'I will consider things often but decide only once.'

'Enthusiasm is attractive and stimulating; I will show it and be loved by others.'

WANING MOON – for letting go, and letting things be:

'I won't hang on to that which won't hang on to me.'

'The eyes believe themselves; the ears only believe others.'

'Magic will happen if I believe in it.'

DARK OF THE MOON – to acknowledge your 'shadow' side:

'I can be heartless, but from that place I discover my heart.'

'I may ask for a lot, but I must take what is offered.'

'I must be sure to recognise what it is I was looking for when I find it.'

SOLAR RETURN SALUTATION – welcoming your new solar year to be true to who you are:

Repeat on your birthday: 'I am now ready to be the fun-loving star in the sky who brings joy to the world. The sea of possibilities is always there, even when hidden by the giant waves of the ocean.'

SUN IN OPPOSITION – learn to be open to the opposite perspective that lies within you:

Repeat when the sun is in Sagittarius: 'My opposite sign is Sagittarius, a sign of risk-taking, spontaneous passion, bursting with fiery enthusiasm. These things are part of my birth-chart, too, so I go to meet them with wonder and excitement and to be all that I am.'

The Gemini Personality

♊

*I know who I WAS when I got up this morning, but I think
I must have been changed several times since then.*
Lewis Carroll, *Alice's Adventures in Wonderland*

Characteristics: Versatile, playful, intuitive, paradoxical,
quick-witted, flattering, changeable, talkative, erratic,
curious, contrary, scattered, mercurial, observant, the
eternal butterfly; juggles with ideas, lifestyle, roles,
routines, has a young-at-heart attitude to life

Symbol: the Twins
Named after the Greek mythological half-brothers,
mortal Castor and the immortal Polydeuces (*Pollux*
in Latin). The 'twins' were known as the Dioscuri,
which means 'sons of Zeus'. In most versions of the
myth, only Polydeuces was Zeus' son, while Castor
was the son of the mortal Spartan king, although
both were born simultaneously to the same mother,
Queen Leda. To ensure they remained together for

ever, Polydeuces persuaded Zeus to share his
immortality with Castor, and so Zeus placed them in
the sky as the constellation Gemini.

Planetary ruler: Mercury

The closest planet to the sun, Mercury is also the
smallest in our solar system, taking only eighty-eight
days to orbit the sun. Rocky, solid and riddled with
craters like the moon, Mercury spins very slowly, and
takes fifty-nine Earth days to complete one full rotation.
If you were born on Mercury, you'd have a birthday
every three months, but you'd only see the sun rise
once every 108 days. As mercurial as you can get!

Astrological Mercury: The god Mercury (and his
Greek counterpart, Hermes) was known as the
messenger of the gods. He could move freely
between heaven, Earth and the underworld.
Mercury's attributes were associated with
boundaries, travel, trade, bridges, crossroads and
magic. In the birth-chart, Mercury describes the way
we communicate, travel, adapt to circumstances and
how we relate to the world around us.

Element: Air

Air signs delight in all forms of communication and
knowledge. They are intellectually curious, intuitive
yet logical, reasonable and have analytical minds.

Their feeling world is uncomfortable and they prefer to live with their heads in the clouds, rather than the messy waters of emotions.

Modality: Mutable
Flexible, creative, spontaneous, quick-thinking, changeable, restless, evasive, disliking order or structure. As with the other Mutable signs, Virgo, Sagittarius and Pisces, Gemini is the go-between of two seasons, in this case from spring to summer.

Body: In astrology, each sign rules various parts of the body. Gemini traditionally rules the lungs, nervous system, arms and shoulders.

Crystal: Citrine

Sun-sign profile: Born under the sign of the Twins, it's hardly surprising that Geminis have two sides to their personalities (and sometimes more when they're role playing). One is the bubbly, playful, fun-loving twin who wants to be everyone's friend and can adapt to any circumstances. The other, let's say, hidden, darker twin is notorious for their ever-changing mind, and being distracted by anything other than what they're doing now. In fact, while Geminis can pick anyone's brains and wade through a million books on how to do this and that in their quest for knowledge, they find it very hard to truly know who they are themselves. Their lifelong quest is to understand the disparate sides of their personalities and to create a wholeness and unity by accepting this double self.

Your best-kept secret: Hermes, the Greek equivalent of Gemini's ruling god and planet, Mercury, was valued for his dual nature. He is the perfect role model for Gemini self-care. As the treasured messenger of the gods, he moved freely between heaven, the Earth and the underworld. He was clever, dextrous and wise, even though he was also associated with thieves, liars, tricksters and conjurors. He invented the lyre, stole Apollo's cattle and his serpent-entwined magic wand, the caduceus, could send people into a trance-like sleep or wake them from one. Use Gemini's innate duality, just like Hermes' magic wand, as a gift to calm your busy mind yet awaken to your true self.

What gives you meaning and purpose in life? Being young at heart, knowing about everything. Observing life, Nature; play, creativity, writing, wit, art, words, moving ever onwards.

What makes you feel good to be you? Knowledge, talking, intelligent partners, variety, travel, change, new ideas, having two phones, two laptops, two names, two loves, two lifestyles; flirtatious fun; reading everything there is to be read, even the labels on your shoes

What or who do you identify with? Gemini identifies with travellers, writers and a young-at-heart attitude. Characters such as Peter Pan or fantasy worlds such as *Through the Looking-Glass, and What Alice Found There*, where life is filled with imagination, curious questions, paradoxes and cryptic answers. Geminis want to be recognised for their ability to adapt to any circumstances, but most of all to be understood and accepted for their light-hearted take on life.

What stresses you out? Demands, commitment, orders, sticking to the rules, being told what to do, control freaks, traffic jams, boredom, not having a phone

What relaxes you? Fun-loving people, crosswords, puzzles, playing games, jokes, Nature, walking, quick fitness programmes, bookshops, all kinds of reading – whether self-help, romance, intrigue, history or non-fiction; light-hearted chatter, your wandering mind

What challenges you? Gemini's greatest challenge is sticking to routines. Although you may try out all kinds of fitness regimes or makeovers to stay 'eternally young', you quickly get bored with them. Being bound and tied to any kind of commitment or time scale, inevitably clashes with Gemini's need for freedom.

What Does Self-Care Mean For Gemini?

To conjure self-care into your life, open up to the Gemini paradox: the only routine you need is to have *no* set routines. However, Gemini does need a wide range of possible options from which to choose. That way, you can feed yourself on self-care knowledge – and the more you know, the better you'll feel about the choices open to you. The following pages will bring you all the best playful rituals and exercises to suit your mercurial mind, enhance and relax your speedy metabolism and boost your fascination for knowing more about self-care than any other sign.

Self-Care Focus

Gemini has an innate talent for trading ideas and transmitting information. As if blessed with the winged sandals of the god Hermes, you can swoop into conversations and out again, pick up ideas and tips and become an information guru on just about everything. Not specialising in any one subject has led some astrology circles to dub Gemini as 'jack of all trades, master of none'. Yet, it's this very ability to duck and dive in and out of a multitude of subjects and acquire a wide range of knowledge that is one of the best ways to feel good and care for you.

Remember that for you, 'me-time' is play time. So dive into these self-care ideas whenever you're in need of a little 'play time'. Open up the odd window of opportunity when you can, and every time, remind yourself: 'I am looking after me, now'.

Self-care can also work to your advantage when you double up with someone else. You might well enjoy internal chit chat with your imaginary twin (although to you, this twin may seem very real indeed), but why not share your tea ceremony with a pal and make it fun? Play tennis, Scrabble or go for a long walk with a friend, practise yoga together over a video app, talk to a tree or listen to birdsong and join in the chorus.

PART ONE

Caring For Your Mind And Feelings

The love of books is among the choicest gifts of the gods.

Sir Arthur Conan Doyle, writer

his section will inspire you to delight in your thoughts, express your ideas and take pleasure in your feelings. Once you get that deep sense of awareness of who you are and what you need, not only will it feel good to be alive, but you will be even more content to be yourself. The rituals and practices here will boost your self-esteem, motivate you to lead a more serene existence and enhance all forms of relationships with others. The most important relationship of all, with yourself, will be nurtured in the best possible way according to your sun sign.

Here are some ideas, rituals and practices for your brilliant, chattering mind, to help you nurture, inspirit, treasure and love who you are.

Now Geminis have no problem mining the depths of taboo subjects, borrowing and adapting ideas, aligning to the energy of new people and places, trading and transmitting information. You probably write thousands of Post-it notes or lists, read every self-care book under the sun (including astrology ones) and are fascinated to discover that it's ok to have a lifestyle where you double up on everything. This can include having two mobile phones, two laptops, two jobs, two nicknames, two identities, two homes and so on. However, while gathering vast quantities of knowledge on the way, and saying, 'Well, at least I know everything that's out there', you may still worry (a Gemini niggle) that you're not 'doing enough' to care for yourself.

Even though the Air signs are considered 'thinking signs', that doesn't mean they don't have feelings or emotions; rather, it means that they tend to avoid or escape them whenever they can. Caring for your feelings means learning to accept you can feel sad, happy, loving, angry – and it's not as scary as you think. Feelings, like thoughts, come and then go. The rituals and practices in this section will enable you to take time to befriend, accept and acknowledge your feelings, providing opportunities to pamper your versatile mind, flow into calm, nurture your feelings and be at one with you.

A DAILY MANTRA

✳

As a daily ritual may prove more like hard work than fun, use this affirmation to start yourself off on your self-care journey. Say it every day, and that's really all you'll need to embark on whatever self-care ritual or exercise you care to choose:

Self-care is fun time, so when the moment comes, I'll say, 'Hey, it's time to play'.

. . . .

JOURNALING

✳

Gemini journaling practice uses two books – one for the eternally youthful, 'butterfly childlike' you, the other for the ordinary, 'I'm-just-a-human-being' you. You are going to name one journal 'The Magical Me' and the other 'The Ordinary Me'.

'The Magical Me' journal is for beautiful words, poetry, imaginative ideas, the joy of observing a bird, listing what brings you joy, expressing the childlike exuberance of the divine in you, sketching or scribbling rhymes or notes.

'The Ordinary Me' journal is to fill with daily thoughts, lists, plans, logic, organised thoughts – in fact, all the stuff you may prevaricate about, but which may help to organise and prioritise your lifestyle.

Together, the two journals will allow you to meet yourself with more acceptance and self-awareness and enjoy discovering more about who you really are. It's a great way to exercise your mind and, at the same time, care for your dual nature.

You will need:
* A candle
* 2 journals or notebooks
* 2 clear quartz crystals

1. Light the candle for atmosphere and place the two journals side by side on the table in front of you.

2. Place one crystal on each book, and then say the following affirmation to seal your intention for using these books to care for yourself and your mind: 'I am becoming who I am, and with these journals I will accept, care for and love all of myself'.

3. Take up the crystals, hold one in each hand and repeat the affirmation twice more.

4. Put the crystals aside, and blow out the candle.

Now you have established a connection to the books, it's time to write your first words.

In 'The Magical Me' journal, write a list of, say, ten things that bring you joy. For example:

1. Light-hearted conversation

2. Being free to do as I please

3. Listening to music

4. Chatting on the phone

In 'The Ordinary Me' journal, write a list of another ten things you don't like or think are not very interesting about you. For example:

* My indifference to others' feelings
* The way I get distracted
* My impatience
* Being just another face in the crowd

Keep your journals close to hand and, whenever you feel the need to record or note something you delight in, love or are fed up with, write in the one you feel is most appropriate. As you gradually build up your journals, stick in images, quotes and ideas to help nourish your mind. You can also make notes on your practices or record how you feel after trying out any of the rituals in this book.

CURIOSITY CARDS

♡

Mental stimulation is essential to Gemini's wellbeing. So why not create a deck of 'curiosity cards' and whenever you're in need of a burst of fun inspiration, draw a card from the deck and follow the signpost . . .

You will need:

* A deck of cards you don't mind scribbling on; or, better still, make your own cards using an online template (see Resources, p. 117), which you can cut out from thick paper – the benefit of this approach is that you can add and discard ideas when you like)

* A pen

1. Start off by writing down on each card a word that sums up things you are curious to know more about – for example, cooking, birds, astrology, sex, crystals, origami, medicine or whatever. You might find as you write on each card that you think, Ooh, I'd like to do that now! But finish your set of cards first – there could be ten or twenty or more – it's up to you and whenever you have run out of ideas.

2. Next, simply shuffle your cards, focus on the moment and pick a card from the deck. Turn it over and enjoy researching, engaging or getting to know more about the curiosity you have picked for the day, week or even for just an hour.

This practice is food for the Gemini soul, and it means you care about the curious nature of you. You can remove or add cards or even create a whole new set whenever the mood takes you.

DESTRESS RITUAL

Like most Geminis, you have deadlines, meetings, work that needs attention, a pile of ironing to get through – and if you don't get on with it, it will stress you out. Use this simple ritual any time you feel overwhelmed or stressed about getting things done – it will put you in the right frame of mind to just do it.

You will need:
* A clear quartz or any favourite crystal
* A small pouch
* A paper and pencil

1. Hold the crystal and say the following affirmation: 'I know I have to get organised, so I'll write down a list of priorities, times and dates, and by caring about that, I will be nurtured.'

2. Now hold the crystal to your forehead or third-eye chakra (see p. 20) and, just for twenty seconds, breathe in and out slowly, counting each in- and each out-breath to find stillness.

3. Place the crystal beside you and write down a list of what you have to do and when.

Keep the crystal in a pouch and carry it with you. Perform the above ritual whenever you need to calm that overthinking Gemini mind.

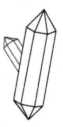

TRAIN OF THOUGHT

✳

It's easy for Geminis to get distracted by the many fascinating things there are to think about. But to put your erratic 'train of thought' back on track, try creating a sanctuary – a place where you can go and let your mind do some wandering for a while before returning to any specific plan.

You will need:

* A place where you can leave the items below all year round
* A clear quartz double-terminator (see Glossary, p. 119) crystal – i.e. one with two points
* A pile of books (or magazines, papers – anything with a lot of words)
* A pen and paper or journal

1. Hold the crystal between your hands with the points facing away from and towards you.

2. Close your eyes and say, 'My mind may wander, but my train of thought visits many places, and so here I will stay and be amused for a while'.

3. Place the crystal on the table, and take up any book, magazine or paper. As you glance through the pages, write down in your journal or on your piece of paper any word or phrase that attracts your attention or 'stands out', free-associating the words in your head, letting that train of thought run freely, without tracks, without a destination. Do this for as long or as short a time as you like.

Once you have let your mind run free, you'll see how easy it is to get back on track and heading in the right direction.

....

EMBRACE YOUR CAREFREE SELF

♡

Geminis are often accused of being too carefree. Yet being carefree doesn't mean you are free of care – that you don't care about others. You *do* care about the world; it's just that you find it hard to show it in the way that is expected of you.

Here's a simple ritual to harness your carefree spirit in a positive way.

You will need:
* A candle
* A handful of pebbles or polished tumbled stones

1. Light the candle and place all the stones in front of it. It doesn't matter how many you have – what is important is what you do next.

2. One by one, pick up the stones and for each one repeat:
> This stone is free and easy
> This stone is carefree
> This stone lets me both *care* and be *free*.

3. Replace each stone on the table after you have said the above.

4. Once you have picked up and replaced each stone and connected to them, thank them for being part of your world, where being carefree doesn't mean you don't care.

Practising this ritual every new moon will help you to maintain your carefree spirit and remind you that you care for the Universe, too.

BEEHIVE VISUALISATION

With buzzing thoughts like busy bees around a hive, sometimes you need to get your mind in order, to give you time to relax and enjoy just being, without thinking. The following visualisation should help with this:

1. Imagine hundreds of worker bees leaving their hive as the morning sun rises.

2. Picture them as they go in search of their favourite flowers for pollen and nectar.

3. Then imagine them returning, with the evening sun, humming and buzzing as they make their way back to the hive in time for sundown to share their delights with the queen bee.

4. As the bees enter the hive, imagine they are your thoughts being stored away in an orderly fashion. Now you can relax and just be, ready to greet the sun another day.

Try this whenever you feel overwhelmed by your busy thoughts and just want to chill out and be you.

....

THE REAL ME

*

We all wonder 'Who is the real me?' sometimes, whatever sign we are. But like the twins of the zodiac, Gemini has two distinct sides to their personality (the magical twin and the ordinary twin – remember?), so you're actually searching for two 'real mes' who make up the one 'me'.

Here's a little exercise to help you love both 'twins':

You will need:
* Pen and paper
* A piece of rose quartz

1. On your piece of paper, draw the astrological symbol of the Twins (or just two stick people).

2. Write the following affirmations below the symbol:
'My dual nature makes me at one with the Universe.'
'I love all of myself, and who I am becoming.'
'Self-awareness brings me joy.'
'The real me is authentic, grateful and loving.'

3. Now just sit calmly for about five minutes and wonder at the 'real' you. Focus on the affirmations on the paper, and you will begin to connect to both your twins and understand their different ways of looking at life: the magical twin always looking for inspiration; the ordinary twin always prevaricating.

Fold up the paper and place the piece of rose quartz on top of it. Leave the paper and crystal on a window ledge or somewhere that is exposed to the sun and moon for one lunar cycle to reinforce your love for your twin self.

....

YOUR INNER CHILD

♡

The more people insist that Geminis 'grow up', the less likely they are to do so. After all, being grown up is a challenge for the eternally young Gemini spirit.

Why not try this exercise whenever you feel pressurised by the demands of adult life?

You will need:
* A mirror
* 2 candles – 1 white, 1 red
* A felt-tip pen/wax crayon or lipstick to write on the mirror (non-indelible)

1. Sit before your mirror and light the two candles, placing them either side of it.

2. Now gaze at your reflection and start to talk out loud, as if addressing your inner child. You can say anything you want, but kindness speaks loudest to the child within, so try, 'Bless you. I'm really grateful for my eternally youthful self, and how you bring me alive when I need you.'

3. Then write on the mirror: 'I care about the child within', 'I care about myself' and lastly, 'I care about who I am, both the child and the adult'.

This practice is perfect for reminding you to respect and nurture that child within.

....

WHISPER TO THE BIRDS

✦✦
✦

As an Air sign, Gemini resonates with the magic of birds. It doesn't matter whether it's a lark, a robin, a swallow or a dove – there is a mysterious connection between the birds of the sky and the free bird of the zodiac. When you see a bird winging through the air, don't you wish you could fly? Geminis often have lucid dreams that they can fly; if you do, it's a sign that you are beginning to understand your true nature.

This little ritual will give you a twitter of happiness every time you voice your joy to the birds above.

1. Stroll out one morning and look up at the sky. If you don't see any birds, it doesn't matter; just know that they are there. You may not hear them either, but do sound or sight actually exist unless someone is listening or seeing? Reflect on this.

2. Next, sing, whistle or whisper any words you like to the birds, the sky and the clouds. Whisper kindness and delight in revealing yourself to Nature; embrace the joy of feeling as free as the birds, and they will eventually reply. You only have to listen, and somewhere, through the silence, you will hear a chirp, birdsong or a whoosh of wings. Watch the birds watching you and the world, and you know that you are caring for them, as they care for you.

Try this ritual whenever you are in need of an uplifting moment or to lighten your day.

Relationships

Gregarious and flirtatious, Geminis' carefree attitude to life doesn't do them many favours when it comes to long-term partnerships. This bright and breezy approach to love is often misunderstood as glib or uncaring. You adore all the romantic trimmings of love, as long as you can maintain your independence and some freedom. But behind that restless, ever-changing persona is a soft and gentle heart. Gemini love is gentle, light and airy; it thrives on friendship first, mutual goals and plans second, sensual bliss and dark passion last.

Love relationships that are fun, entertaining, changeable, unconditional and don't tie you down to monotony or routines will keep you committed. The last thing you want from a relationship is to be smothered, mothered or told what to do. You need to travel, get out and about and socialise and do your own thing whenever you feel so inclined. Gemini is one of the most generous and kind-hearted of lovers – as long as your partner gives you enough room to express your independent spirit.

Try the practices below to improve all forms of love relationships, and to nurture your own Gemini love expression.

IMAGINE ALL THE WORLD FEELING AT ONCE

✳

In the big wide world, we all have emotions. At some point in our lives, we all probably experience hope, despair, love, care, desire, compassion and so on. Some zodiac signs can deal with the feeling world better than others, such as Scorpio, who relies on what they feel to understand both their own and others' motives. The trouble for you, as a Gemini, is that you are a light-hearted Air sign, and so you unconsciously avoid situations that may involve you feeling too much. Here is a visualisation that will enable you to see that feelings are common to us all, even unwelcome ones.

* Sit somewhere comfortable, where you can find soli-tude and stillness.
* Imagine all the people in all the world feeling joy, including you.
* Now imagine all the people in the world feeling hope, including you.
* Next, imagine all the people in the world feeling sad, including you.
* Be aware of all the people in the world both feeling

61

and thinking and realise how you are not alone and all is one.

Whenever you sense a moment of resistance to your feelings, do this little visualisation exercise to remind you it's ok to feel.

LAW OF ATTRACTION

✳

You wouldn't be the Gemini you are if you didn't enjoy flirting, dating, having fun with your partner or seducing a few strangers. Caring about your fun side is just as important to your wellbeing as caring about the more serious side. So why not use a little witchy magic to get your way and attract someone new (or someone you want to get to know better) into your life?

You will need:
* A length of red twine or ribbon (about 60cm or 24 inches)
* A mirror
* A garnet or ruby (to attract love and passion)
* A pen and paper

1. Wind the ribbon into a circle in front of the mirror.

2. Place the garnet or ruby in the centre of the circle.

3. To activate the charm, write on the piece of paper:
New romance (or close connection) is mine to see,
With this charm they'll come to me.

4. Now look into the mirror and say the charm as you hold out the garnet or ruby to your reflection.

5. Fold the paper and place it somewhere safe, so you can reuse it another time, if desired.

Carry your garnet with you wherever you go and a new or recent love interest will soon be swooning at the sight of you.

EMOTION-WATCHING EXERCISE

Another way for Geminis to acknowledge their love feelings is to simply observe them with their brilliant objectivity. So whenever you feel a wave of desire, excitement or concern, hold on to it, rather than try to resist or send it away: notice the emotion as if you are looking into yourself from the outside; be mindful of how it feels, even if it hurts; be aware of the pain of hurt or the power of desire, too.

If you practise doing this kind of observation from your higher self, you will begin to see how the feeling will whizz off again, like birds winging their way across the sky.

Because 'emotion watching' *is* rather like bird watching and can be a great source of self-knowledge.

An objective approach to feeling will bring you new inspiration, and fresh ways to look at relationships and your love desires.

....

ACCEPTANCE PENTAGRAM

✳

Accepting and caring for others is a lovely way to accept yourself. In fact, if you can share some of your joyful Gemini spirit with those who mean something to you, then the world will be a happier place. Try the following simple ritual during a new crescent-moon phase to enhance all forms of acceptance in your relationship world.

1. Draw or find an image of a pentagram (a five-pointed star) and print or cut it out.

2. Place it so that one point is to the north.

3. In the middle space, write 'Myself and others'.

4. In each of the five surrounding points, going clockwise, write the words: 'Gratitude', 'Integrity', 'Acceptance', 'Value' and 'Kindness'.

5. To activate the power of these qualities, leave in a safe place for at least one lunar cycle.

The magic pentagram will invoke self-love and acceptance and give out love to those you care about, too.

PART TWO

Caring For Your Body

You are – your life, and nothing else.

Jean-Paul Sartre, writer and philosopher

Here, you will discover alternative ways to look after and nurture your body, not just as a physical presence, but its connection to mind and spirit, too. This section gives you a wide range of ideas, from using sun-sign crystals to protect your physical and psychic self to fitness, diet and beauty tips. There are specific chakra practices and yoga poses especially suited to your sun sign, not forgetting bath-time rituals and calming practices to destress and nurture holistic wellbeing.

Some signs, like Virgo, are quite fanatical about getting their bodies in shape, while Air signs like yourself are more concerned with the mind and intellect. So use your mind to tell your body what it needs, and listen to the feedback your body gives you.

Even if you're not up for pole-vaulting or winning Wimbledon, at least make sure you go for a jog, an invigorating walk or a bike ride to clear buzzing thoughts and give your body and respiratory system a good workout. Remember, you can choose a different landscape each time you go out, ensuring that you always have fascinating new scenery to discover, while filling yourself with loads of fresh air to keep your lungs clear and your mind fresh.

As a flirtatious Gemini, you like to look after your outer appearance and make sure it attracts the right kind of attention, so you have little trouble indulging in the odd pampering session when the mood takes you. Gemini is associated with the throat chakra (see p. 87) – an energy centre that balances all forms of communication, as well as radiating speedy thoughts and speedy actions. That young-at-heart soul thrives in a supple, nimble and fleet-footed body, so dip into the wide variety of practices in this section to enhance all aspects of your physical wellbeing.

Fitness and Movement

Gemini rules the lungs, nervous system, arms and shoulders, so your fitness self-care routine is best centred around mindful breathing and easy, fun exercises that don't take up too much of your time. It may seem like a 'nice idea' to join a gym, but once the 'idea' becomes a routine chore, you are likely to give it up and seek out the next new programme. Your best physical-exercise bets are dancing, tennis, badminton, walking or jogging with a friend, or any physical activity involving you and one other player.

....

WALKING MEDITATION

♡

Sitting down to meditate can be a struggle for active, restless Gemini. However, a walking meditation is the perfect way to clear your mind. Focusing on a specific part of your body brings attention to that area, creating a balance between intention and action. Here's a simple way to be mindful of the body and stay active:

Whether you are walking across the countryside or down a street, up a staircase or along a garden path, notice the rhythm of your arms, feet and breathing. Be conscious of the muscles moving in your legs or the spring in your step. Feel the weight shift from one foot to the other. How is your back? Are you walking upright? Are you stooped or unbalanced in any way? Do you swing your arms back and forth in rhythm with your gait, or are they still? Enjoy the walk, the air, the experience. Be aware of yourself and how you interact with the world around you.

In this type of meditation, you are mindfully aware of all the experience, so notice your arms, your head, your neck, and engage in the whole process of walking as it leads you somewhere. It doesn't matter where you're going; the process of being at one with your body will revitalise and animate you. This kind of awareness, on a regular basis, will keep you feeling forever young.

BREATH TRICKS

♡

The following two breathwork practices are perfect ways for Geminis to balance mind and body, enhance deeper awareness and relax their overactive nervous systems while restoring flexibility to the body.

You can do these simple exercises any time. If you feel a bit stressed, the first 'chi breath' exercise will calm you down; or it can be done first thing in the morning as you wake, and last thing at night to help you sleep.

The 'salutation breath' is great for when you are about to go for a walk or do yoga or any other form of physical exercise; it will prepare your body and vitalise and inspirit your mind, too.

Chi breath

The flow of universal energy through all things, known as 'chi' or 'prana', is vital for overall wellbeing. Your lungs are like a pair of swing doors, opening and closing on the invisible energy.

* To maximise air into your lungs, stand or sit straight and breathe purposefully from your lower diaphragm, rather than your upper chest. Notice how your abdomen rises and falls and be mindful of your breath as

you breathe in slowly, and out again through your nose.

* Breathe in to the count of seven, then breathe out to the count of eleven. Continue until you feel relaxed, and all tension will disappear.

* Afterwards, give gratitude to the air you breathe, and mostly to the body that is doing the breathing by saying, 'Thanks for the air I breathe, and thanks to my body and soul'.

Spend two or three sessions a day of say, two minutes each being aware of your breathing to restore and relax your mind and body and vitalise your chakras (see p. 20).

Salutation breath

Taken from a yoga salutation pose, this breathing practice is best done outside in the fresh air, facing the sun, if possible, to harness its power and restore and strengthen all your chakras (see pp. 20 and 87).

1. Stand tall with your hands by your sides, and breathe in slowly while stretching your arms wide

2. Bring your hands into prayer pose (palms facing and touching together) in front of your chest.

3. Next, sweep your arms above your head to high prayer pose (palms together pointing to the sky) and, as you breathe out, return your arms and hands to your sides.

Do five to ten rounds of this practice at a time, at least once a day if you can. As you smile at the sun, you will feel the uplifting benefits to body and soul.

....

YOGA CAT AND COW STRETCH

♡

With a non-stop hunger for writing, networking, being on the internet, walking with phone to ear, mouth to phone and trying to do twenty tasks at once, your neck, back and shoulders need some TLC to prevent stiffness or other problems. One of the best ways to combine spiritual, physical and mental wellbeing is with a regular yoga practice.

This basic yoga pose is easily done at any time of day and will restore good posture and prevent back problems.

* In the table-top position (hands and knees on floor, hips aligned over knees, shoulders over wrists), curl your toes under, and tilt your pelvis so that your tail-bone/bottom sticks up and your belly drops down, shoulders down.
* Gaze up towards the ceiling in this arched cow position.
* Now return your toes to a flat position, drop your head and gaze down at your navel, as you round your back like a cat.
* Repeat one stretch of cat on the inhale and one stretch of cow as you exhale.

* Continue for 5–10 rounds, then go back to the neutral table-top position (hands and knees on the floor, back straight).

Having practised this pose, you will feel aligned, nourished and relaxed, and any stress or tension in your shoulders or neck will improve.

Nutrition

Your fast metabolism quickly gets rid of toxins and fats in your body, which is beneficial for overall health, but because you are so erratic about mealtimes, you often don't eat a balanced diet. As you have little time to study diet plans or count your calories, the key to Gemini wellbeing is to make time to eat between your busy multitasking schedules. With your dislike of routine, it's hardly surprising that set mealtimes can seem a nuisance when you'd rather be doing something more interesting. So if you can't face three big meals a day, try to compromise a little and opt for, say, four or five mini meals a day, all filled with good, nutritious foods.

SLOW DOWN

★★
★

Geminis eat as fast as they think, so try to eat a little more slowly to allow food to process, nutrients to be absorbed and nervous energy to be contained.

To slow your eating down, notice the colour of the food or the taste, describe these senses to yourself, or write them down in your journal. You may begin to realise there is magic in the things you eat, just as there is magic in the things you read or see. By observing your own food habits and the way you eat, you will care more for your body's needs.

....

CREATIVE EATING

Variety is the spice of life for a Gemini, so to help you get creative in the kitchen, try the following:

1. Write a list of the most nutritious and appetising foods you can buy and stick it on your fridge.

2. Make delicious, small meals from the items on your brilliant list (you'll easily source good recipes if you rummage through health magazines and online). You will find more pleasure from eating little and often – whether it's your morning oats (good for Gemini's cognitive processes), fermented foods or exotic delicacies.

The more variety the better, and the more you find time to research food, diets and nutritional health, the more your body will benefit from your findings. Surely that's one more fascinating subject to add to your curiosity cards (see p. 45)!

Beauty

Of course, you like to look youthful, and all forms of beauty therapy are Gemini's best friend. Although you prefer to avoid routine and it can be a chore to put on your make-up every day, once ready, you know it's all worthwhile. So here are a few tips to enhance that young-at-heart persona and give you the chance to indulge in being your beautiful self.

HANDY AFFIRMATION

✳

Mercury, your planetary ruler, governs the hands, so when you're in the mood for a little bit of relaxed pampering, a manicure, finger massage or luxury hand spa gives the greatest care to this most important part of your body.

Repeat this affirmation whenever you are mindful of the beauty of your hands:

I love my hands. They bring me joy in everything I do.

Looking after your hands will not only remind you of your Gemini dexterity, but also show off to the world the care you have for these symbols of self-expression.

GOLD-STAR BATH TIME

✳

Even a high-wired Gemini benefits from a relaxing bath ritual. This will take away the stresses and worries of your busy mind, while instilling a sense of your unique star quality – the realisation that the solar light that shines through you is your personal gold.

You will need:
* 5 gold tea lights
* 5 yellow/orange/gold flower heads (such as marigolds, orange or yellow roses, sunflowers, etc.)
* Rose essential oil
* 5 pieces of citrine or goldstone
* A glass of bubbly, green tea or whatever you enjoy most

1. Place a candle at each corner of your bath, and the fifth in a place of your choice.

2. Run the bath to your preferred level.

3. Place the flower heads carefully on the surface of the water and drizzle a drop of rose oil on to each flower. Don't worry if the flowers sink – it's the intention to place them there that creates the magic.

4. Place a crystal alongside each candle, and light up!

5. Pour yourself a glass of something 'star-worthy', (whatever takes your fancy) and then sink into your bath and bathe by candlelight.

6. As you relax, gaze at one of the candle flames, and imagine you are in the middle of the cosmos, surrounded by all the stars in the night sky. But you are the star that shines the brightest. Relax for as long as you like and reflect on how your body is as beautiful as the heavens. In fact, tell yourself, 'I am a heavenly body', and feel a connection to the solar light within you.

CHAKRA BALANCE

The body's chakras are the epicentres of the life-force energy that flows through all things (see p. 20).

Gemini is mostly associated with the throat chakra of communication. This chakra is concerned with the way we put our messages across, our interaction with the world and how objective or subjective we are.

When this chakra is underactive, you may not have as much to say as usual, or resent other people who seem bright, breezy and more carefree than you are. You may misunderstand what's being said, be unable to express your thoughts or sulk if you're not getting your way. To reinforce and balance this chakra, carry or wear green aventurine to promote fresh ideas and brilliant thinking. Once balanced, inspiration returns, communication skills improve and anything that you need to say will be said with clarity.

If you have an overactive throat chakra, you may be verbose, flippant, won't listen to anyone else and think you know best or have all the answers. You can also be self-opinionated and blame others for your problems. To subdue this energy and restore harmony, carry or wear blue lace agate, symbolising acceptance and understanding of others.

Balancing this chakra will enhance Gemini's physical and mental health, bring you better relationships and improve your successful communication in any business or lifestyle projects.

General Wellbeing

Apart from being mindful of physical health and beauty, Geminis also need to feel protected and in harmony with their environments. So here are some fun practices to promote your general wellbeing, whether to feel empowered, serene or at peace with the world.

SLEEP BOOSTER

♡

Geminis tend towards erratic sleep patterns. Some nights they sleep for twelve hours solidly without waking, on others they may wake several times in the night, as thoughts run wild and their brains go into overdrive.

This recipe will help you sleep peacefully.

You will need:

* A small glass phial or bottle filled with 10 drops of almond oil
* 3 drops of lavender essential oil
* 3 drops of ylang-ylang essential oil
* A basil leaf

1. Drop the essential oils into the almond oil.

2. Crush the basil leaf, sprinkle it into the phial and leave for an hour or so before using.

3. Anoint your bed: a few minutes before you go to bed, dot a little oil on your pillow or the edge of the mattress, and say the following: 'This potion will bring me sweet sleep and dreams, to awaken refreshed with the sun'.

You can also dot a little of the oil on your wrist as you read your favourite book in bed, and you'll be assured of a restful sleep.

SOOTHING THE NERVES

Geminis can be nervy, rushing around and getting in a bit of a tizz if there are too many demands or duties (big hate) thrown in their direction. Of course, you will get it sorted, probably in a disorganised way – you know that. But here's a quick tip for calming your nerves before getting down to business.

Our lips are incredibly sensitive, filled with parasympathetic nerve fibres. Try running your fingers gently from left to right, back and forth across your lips for about thirty seconds (or, if you prefer, apply lip balm). This will soothe your nerves and calm you in preparation for the task ahead.

CRYSTALS FOR CHARISMA

♡

Looking after appearances takes up a lot of time for some signs (you can't imagine how long a Leo takes in the bathroom every day!), but we need to attend to our inner beauty, too. This is the 'thing' that some call 'charisma', others call magic, glamour or bewitchment. Whatever you prefer to call it, you already have it – you just need to unleash it. The following ritual will help to boost your inner charisma.

You will need:
* A piece of citrine
* A piece of rough ruby
* A piece of lapis lazuli
* A piece of tiger's eye
* A glass bowl
* 3 drops of frankincense oil

1. Put all the crystals in the bowl and place it in the south corner of your home.

2. To seal your intention, drizzle the frankincense oil across the stones and say: 'With the power of these crystals I will be charismatic and magical wherever I go.'

3. Leave overnight, and from then on, each time you go out, randomly pick a crystal to take with you, to dazzle and impress. (Don't forget to put it back in the bowl when you come home.)

By following this practice in your home, you will highlight that inner magic that makes you so irresistible.

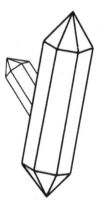

....

TEA CEREMONY FOR HAPPY DAYS

♡

A tea ceremony is a traditional Japanese ritual for serenity and wellbeing. You can do this with a friend or alone.

You will need:

* A teapot
* 2 teaspoons of loose-leaf green tea
* A crumbled lemon verbena or lemon-balm leaf
* A teaspoon

1. Make the tea and crumble in the leaf.

2. As you do so, be mindful of the leaf itself, the colour of the tea, the cup, the teapot.

3. Watch the leaves swirl, as you stir once with a teaspoon, then let them settle at the bottom of the cup.

4. Wait for a few minutes, then begin to sip the tea and visualise what happiness means to you. It will very soon manifest in your life.

This ritual will restore your Gemini spirit and remind you that light-heartedness is the key to happiness.

PART THREE

Caring For Your Soul

When you do things from your soul,
you feel a river moving in you, a joy.

Rumi, thirteenth-century Persian poet

This final section offers you tailored, fun, easy and amazing ways to connect to and care for your sacred self. This, in turn, means you will begin to feel at one with the joyous energy of the Universe. You don't have to sign up to any religion or belief system (unless you want to) – just take some time to experience uplifting moments through your interaction with the spiritual aspects of the cosmos. Care for your sun sign's soul centre, and you care about the Universe, too.

Like the other Air signs, Libra and Aquarius, your innate thirst for knowledge includes all things spiritual. Your curiosity takes you on many different journeys to discover alternative beliefs, such as Hermeticism (associated with Hermes and the Egyptian god of magic and wisdom, Thoth), Wicca (a form of modern paganism), or pleasurable inspiration in spiritual poets such as Rumi and Kahlil Gibran.

Although you can come across as flippant about 'enlightenment' or glib about attaching oneself to a 'guru figure', you know deep within that there is something numinous at work. Your divine twin is well connected to the unconscious realms and beyond. In fact, the great joy you find in Nature, or the creative urge that 'takes you out of yourself', stems from this secret place within – a place where you can rest a while from the busy chattering of your mind. On the surface (and particularly when young), Geminis appear lonely, always searching for something or someone, but as they grow older, they find their greatest joy in solitude – simply because they know they are not alone at all.

The following rituals and practices will align you with this secret place within yourself, so you can enjoy discovering your connection to the Universe, while caring for that sacredness, too.

Symbolic Language

Many Geminis make great linguists; they pick up foreign languages quickly, and don't rely on traditional teaching methods, often understanding what's being said purely by the resonance or rhythm of the spoken word.

Similarly, the language of symbols is a way to connect to the sacredness within you. Arcane or mysterious symbols and signs provide insight into the workings of the Universe, and you'll be in your element decoding symbolic imagery. It will also give you a deep understanding of the hidden languages of the Universe itself. Start off by working with the simple but ingenious symbol of infinity as described in the next exercise.

....

UNICURSAL HEXAGRAM

If the Universe is about 'all that is', then the unicursal hexagram – a six-pointed star that can be drawn with a single line – will connect you more closely to the unity of All. In many mystical and esoteric beliefs, this symbol represents the power of One, or the divine. Use it to achieve a closer connection to your sacred self.

You will need:
* A pen or pencil
* Some rough paper
* A special piece of paper or your journal
* An image of the hexagram
* Six offerings (for example, a flower, a crystal, a candle, a fallen leaf)

1. Draw the hexagram in one continuous line, copying the image and/or practising on rough paper a few times to get the flow right.

2. Once you feel confident enough, draw the symbol on your special paper or in your journal.

3. Trace your finger along the complete line six times (the number of star points) to seal your intention for profound awareness.

4. Finally, place an offering on each of the points – this can be the same thing for each point or something different, if you like. Be mindful of the hexagram's unified geometry, and focus on you as an individual, as part of the geometrical wholeness of the Universe, too.

5. Fold the paper away and leave it (or your journal) in a safe place.

Perform this ritual whenever you feel the desire to enhance your connection to that special soul place.

NATURE'S CHILD

✳

Wondering at the clouds, gazing up at the stars and being fascinated by the blue tit cracking open a sunflower seed are all ways you like to engage with the divine in Nature as a Gemini. In fact, this enchantment with the world enables you to engage in the magic of the Universe.

Try this simple practice whenever you have time to go out in the countryside, the garden or a green space, where you can 'wander lonely . . .' – as only a Gemini can.

1. Raise your arms to the sky and then bring them down level with your eyes, hands outstretched, as if to hug the landscape into you.

2. Make a hug shape into the visual image of the landscape and literally, in the air in front of you, hug all that is before you.

3. Say:
> My sacred self is connected to this Earth and all the
> Universe.
> To love each cloud, each bird, each star, which
> connects me to the divine in me.

4. Embrace the world for about a minute and repeat the affirmation three more times.

5. Gently return your arms to your sides and bow your head in gratitude for your connection.

You will experience a sense of the divine within yourself with this practice, as well as a positive outlook on the world and your future.

....

PRACTISE MUDRAS

♡

With the gift of dexterity and your excellent hand-eye coordination, the Vedic mudras (symbolic or ritual hand gestures often used in meditation and yoga) are a superb channel to access the spiritual you. These can be performed anywhere and at any time to reinforce your belief or to bring you closer to your sacred self.

To align mind and spirit, use the two mudras below – *hakini* and *chin* – in succession. *Hakini* promotes concentration and in-depth working of the mind, while *chin* brings into harmony the mind, body, spirit and Universe.

Hakini

1. Sit before a table and place your elbows on it, palms together in front of you.
2. Move the palms gently apart, until only the tips of all fingers are touching.
3. Focus on the shape you have created between your hands for a moment, then close your eyes as you imagine awakening the spiritual light between your palms.
4. Hold this pose for, say, two minutes. Then move on to *chin*.

Chin

1. With both hands simultaneously, touch forefingers to thumbs.

2. Let your other fingers spread out and around widely.

You can practise these mudras anywhere and at any time to balance and bring harmony to spirit and mind.

....

SPIRITUAL HANDIWORK

✦✦
✦

As your ruler, Mercury is associated with the hands – why not try a little palmistry (palm reading) or chiromancy, as it's also known, to dig deeper into your true nature?

Chiromancy has been around for thousands of years and has many correspondences to astrology. Various parts of the hand, fingers and palm are associated with the planets. Your ruler, Mercury, corresponds to the mount of Mercury, a fleshy pad located at the base of your third and little finger.

To enhance creativity and to be clear about your chosen direction, gently massage this fleshy pad in a clockwise direction with the thumb of your other hand for a minute or so, then switch hands and repeat the massage. You will soon get the results you desire.

Hand study

By studying the lines on your hands, you can discover what kind of vocation, love or lifestyle suits you best.

Below is a fast-track interpretation to the main lines on your hand to help sharpen your divination skills.

* **The heart line** runs across the top of the palm from the outer edge beneath the little finger and either

curves or runs straight across the palm inwards. It reveals all about your love life – the stronger and longer, the more love relationships play a key part in your life. The shorter or lighter the line – well, then romance is fine, but you're not the commitment type.

* **The head line** is found between the heart and life lines. It describes creative abilities and outlook on life. A strong line means you're incredibly creative, methodical and get the job done; a short line means you find it hard to make decisions or to complete tasks.

* **The life line** forms an arc around the base of the thumb, starting between the index finger and the thumb and ending near the wrist. A strong line shows you're vibrant and energetic; a weak or short line shows that you're more of a bookworm than a sports person.

* **The fate line** runs up the middle of the palm and ends beneath the fingers. It reveals your career direction and motivation. A strong Fate line shows you're dedicated and ambitious; a weak one shows that you need a low-pressure environment in which to flourish.

Divination is about understanding the symbolic language of the Universe, which will enable you to make choices for your future.

STOREHOUSE OF ALL KNOWLEDGE

✳

Another good way for your curious Gemini mind to understand more about this universal energy is to visualise a 'Storehouse of All Knowledge', where all there is to be known is known.

1. Close your eyes and imagine you are travelling down an empty road, perhaps in the middle of nowhere, and you come across a mysterious door on which is written: 'Welcome to the Storehouse of All Knowledge'. Another sign on the door says, 'Free entry. Silence.'

2. You climb the steps and open the door to the great library.

3. As you sit down in the silent place, surrounded by millions of books above, beyond, below and all around you, in among the shelves a golden light shines on a title: *A Book of Secrets For You*. The library is filled with all knowledge of past, present and future, and the recurring motifs, themes and symbols of the collective unconscious – these being the ideas, beliefs and archetypes we all have in common. Yet each individual is designated their own book of secrets.

4. Reflect for a moment on how we all share the same archetypal qualities in life, but each of us must find our own personal book of secrets to discover who we are and how this potential will manifest in our life.

5. Before you open your eyes, notice that you now have a library ticket and it is your right to visit the storehouse at any time. Here you can understand the divine nature of the Universe and get to know yourself better.

Perform this visualisation whenever you need a break from the busy babbling of your Gemini mind, to restore your intuitive and sacred connection.

....

TRUST YOUR INTUITION

♡

As a Gemini, you are often overwhelmed by rational thoughts and overthinking, so that hunches or 'gut feelings' get lost in the busy, jumbled messages of your mind. Your sixth sense is another important gateway to the sacred self and beyond. That's why learning to listen to and act on this inner 'voice' will help you to care about that frequently overlooked part of you. Here's a short visualisation exercise to open the gateway:

1. Sit in a quiet place, close your eyes and visualise a golden glass ball, filled with the mysterious quality of intuition. This golden glass lies in the core of you, maybe just behind your navel or at the base of the spine. Wherever you think it 'sits', imagine 'feeling' it there.

2. See the ball moving up to your mind, creating a glow throughout you, filling every cell and every thought with its golden power.

3. Visualise the ball as the moment you get a hunch, leading you to the right pathway, direction or answer.

4. Come out of your visualisation when you feel ready, open your eyes, and keep the notion of the golden ball with you in your mind.

Whenever your rational mind attempts to take over your intuitive voice, stop, just for a few seconds, and imagine the golden glass ball rising up to give you the answer you know is true.

. . . .

KINDNESS FOR ALL

★★
★

Being kind to your Gemini self is one way you can care for the rest of the world; and being kind to the world means your kind thoughts will generate loving kindness back.

In Buddhist meditation, 'metta' is a loving-kindness practice you can do any time, just by sitting in a still place and thinking mindfully.

1. Find a quiet place and relax.

2. Think about the people, animals, places and ideas you love most in the world (including yourself) and visualise them.

3. Now extend your kindness to all of Nature and all of humanity – even the spider you may fear and the people you think you dislike.

4. Let your feelings of kindness arise within you, then imagine you are hugging or embracing all plants, trees, animals, friends, ideas, rivals, spiders . . . and you are giving out this gentleness, not giving in to your fears.

5. You are now embracing all that is, including you.

Having done this practice, you are ready to walk with the Universe, and know it cares for you, too.

Last Words

The Gemini-born Irish poet W. B. Yeats was one of the most influential literary figures of the twentieth century. Through his artist's eyes he saw the mystery of the world and cared about it deeply. Like his ruling god, Hermes, his mercurial mind plundered the depths of the Earth, rising again to the heavens to bring some of the most poignant and meaningful messages to light.

Yet Gemini is the sign of the Twins, one of whom is magical, light-hearted, flirtatious and funny, while the other has trouble being just an ordinary human being, longing to understand the profound truths of their deepest self. Trying to balance and harmonise these two 'natures' is what Gemini self-care is all about, so you can love yourself and all the potentials that are part of you.

In fact, once you feed your mind with inspired ideas, communicate and transmit your thoughts and enjoy that young-at-heart outlook on life, then you will be caring for both twins. Once you remember to care for your body and outer beauty, then you will be nurturing the physical magic of yourself. Once you start to look after for your inner spiritual beauty, then you'll begin to realise that you can shine your light inside and see your divine connection – and care about that, too. And once you accept that you thrive on 'airy' relationships, where you have space and freedom to be you, you will be a happier, more loving and lovable person who can juggle with the two sides of their personality and enjoy both, as one.

Uplifted and inspired by all aspects of caring for yourself, your authentic Gemini self will shine through, and your life will become more fulfilled in all ways. As Yeats put it:

> The world is full of magic things, patiently waiting for our senses to grow sharper.

Take this to heart and enjoy caring for the person you truly are.

Resources

Main sites for crystals, stones, candles, smudging sticks, incense, pouches, essential oils and everything needed for the holistic self-care practices included in this book:
holisticshop.co.uk
thepsychictree.co.uk
thesoulangels.co.uk
earthcrystals.com
livrocks.com
artisanaromatics.com

For a substantial range of books (and metaphysical items) on astrology, divination, runes, palmistry, tarot and holistic health, etc.:
thelondonastrologyshop.com
watkinsbooks.com
mysteries.co.uk
barnesandnoble.com
innertraditions.com

For more information on astrology, personal horo-
scopes and birth-chart calculations:
astro-charts.com (simplest, very user friendly)

horoscopes.astro-seek.com
(straightforward)
astrolibrary.org/free-birth-chart
(easy to use, with lots of extra information)

Glossary

Aura An invisible electromagnetic energy field that emanates from and surrounds all living beings

Auric power The dominant colour of the aura, which reveals your current mood or state

Chakra Sanskrit for 'wheel', in Eastern spiritual traditions, the seven chakras are the main epicentres – or wheels – of invisible energy throughout the body

Dark of the moon This is when the moon is invisible to us, due to its proximity to the sun; it is a time for reflection, solitude and a deeper awareness of oneself

Divination Gaining insight into the past, present and future using symbolic or esoteric means

Double-terminator crystal A quartz crystal with a point at each end, allowing its energy to flow both ways

Full moon The sun is at its maximum opposition to the moon, thus casting light across all of the moon's orb; in esoteric terms, it is a time for culmination, finalising deals, committing to love and so on

Geopathic stress Negative energy emanating from and on the Earth, such as underground water courses, tunnels, overhead electrical cables and geological faults

Grid A specific pattern or layout of items symbolising specific intentions or desires

Horoscope An astrological chart or diagram showing the position of the sun, moon and planets at the time of any given event, such as the moment of somebody's birth, a marriage or the creation of an enterprise; it is used to interpret the characteristics or to forecast the future of that person or event

New crescent moon A fine sliver of crescent light that appears curving outwards to the right in the northern hemisphere and to the left in the southern hemisphere; this phase is for beginning new projects, new romance, ideas and so on

Psychic energy One's intuition, sixth sense or instincts, as well as the divine, numinous or magical power that flows through everything

Shadow side In astrology, your shadow side describes those aspects of your personality associated with your opposite sign and of which you are not usually aware

Smudging Clearing negative energy from the home with a smouldering bunch of dried herbs, such as sage

Solar return salutation A way to give thanks and welcome the sun's return to your zodiac sign once a year (your birthday month)

Sun in opposition The sun as it moves through the opposite sign to your own sun sign

Sun sign The zodiac sign through which the sun was moving at the exact moment of your birth

Waning moon The phase of the moon after it is full, when it begins to lose its luminosity – the waning moon is illuminated on its left side in the northern hemisphere, and on its right side in the douthern hemisphere; this is a time for letting go, acceptance and preparing to start again

Waxing moon The phase between a new and a full moon, when it grows in luminosity – the waxing moon is illuminated on its right side in the northern hemisphere and on its left side in the southern hemisphere; this is a time for putting ideas and desires into practice

Zodiac The band of sky divided into twelve segments (known as the astrological signs), along which the paths of the sun, the moon and the planets appear to move

About the Author

After studying at the Faculty of Astrological Studies in London, the UK, Sarah gained the Diploma in Psychological Astrology – an in-depth 3-year professional training programme cross-fertilised by the fields of astrology and depth, humanistic and transpersonal psychology. She has worked extensively in the media as astrologer for titles such as *Cosmopolitan* magazine (UK), *SHE, Spirit & Destiny* and the *London Evening Standard*, and appeared on UK TV and radio shows, including *Steve Wright in the Afternoon* on BBC Radio 2.

Her mainstream mind-body-spirit books include the international bestsellers, *The Tarot Bible, The Little Book of Practical Magic* and *Secrets of the Universe in 100 Symbols*.

Sarah currently practises and teaches astrology and other esoteric arts in the heart of the countryside.

Acknowledgements

I would first like to thank everyone at Yellow Kite, Hodder & Stoughton and Hachette UK who were part of the process of creating this series of twelve zodiac self-care books. I am especially grateful to Carolyn Thorne for the opportunity to write these guides; Anne Newman for her editorial advice, which kept me 'carefully' on the right track; and Olivia Nightingall who kept me on target for everything else! It is when people come together with their different skills and talents that the best books are made – so I am truly grateful for being part of this team.

See the full Astrology Self-Care series here

9781399704885   9781399704915   9781399704588

9781399704618   9781399704649   9781399704670

9781399704700   9781399704731   9781399704762

9781399704793   9781399704823   9781399704854

yellow
kite

books to help you live a good life

Join the conversation and tell
us how you live a #goodlife

🐦 @yellowkitebooks
📘 YellowKiteBooks
📌 Yellow Kite Books
📷 YellowKiteBooks